# Prescription for Salvation

Distilling the experience of a lifetime in this
urgent and penetrating book, Dr. Jung affirms

## Other MENTOR Books of Special Interest

☐ **PSYCHOPATHOLOGY OF EVERYDAY LIFE by Sigmund Freud.** The celebrated analyst's easily understood explanation of the hidden causes of everyday errors.                    (#MT755—75¢)

☐ **GESTALT PSYCHOLOGY by Wolfgang Kohler.** A classic statement of the basic concepts of a psychological theory which has profoundly influenced the progress and direction of modern psychology.                    (#MT644—75¢)

☐ **A PRIMER OF FREUDIAN PSYCHOLOGY by Calvin S. Hall.** An easy-to-understand volume giving Freud's thinking on the dynamics and development of the normal personality. (#MT684—75¢)

☐ **PSYCHOLOGY OF SEX by Havelock Ellis.** This precedent-shattering book has been called "the best one-volume treatment of sex in the English language."—Carl Van Doren.    (#MT760—75¢)

---

# C. G. JUNG

# THE UNDISCOVERED SELF

Translated from the German by R. F. C. Hull

MENTOR A MENTOR BOOK

Published by THE NEW AMERICAN LIBRARY,
New York and Toronto

*Published as a MENTOR BOOK*
*by arrangement with Little, Brown and Company,*
*by whom the work is published in association*
*with the Atlantic Monthly Press.*
*A hardcover edition is available from*
*Little, Brown and Company.*

A portion of this book first appeared in the Centennial issue
of the *Atlantic*.


SEVENTH PRINTING


MENTOR TRADEMARK REG. U.S. PAT. OFF. AND FOREIGN COUNTRIES
REGISTERED TRADEMARK—MARCA REGISTRADA
HECHO EN CHICAGO, U.S.A.

MENTOR BOOKS are published *in the United States* by
The New American Library, Inc.,
1301 Avenue of the Americas, New York, New York 10019,
*in Canada* by The New American Library of Canada Limited,
295 King Street East, Toronto 2, Ontario

PRINTED IN THE UNITED STATES OF AMERICA

*To my friend*
*Fowler McCormick*

This book was prompted by conversations between Dr. Jung and Dr. Carleton Smith, director of the National Arts Foundation, which brought it to the attention of the editors of the Atlantic Monthly Press.

# CONTENTS

# I

## THE PLIGHT OF THE INDIVIDUAL
## IN MODERN SOCIETY

WHAT WILL THE FUTURE BRING? FROM TIME IM-
memorial this question has occupied men's
minds, though not always to the same degree.
Historically, it is chiefly in times of physical,
political, economic and spiritual distress that
men's eyes turn with anxious hope to the future, and when anticipations, utopias and
apocalyptic visions multiply. One thinks, for
instance, of the chiliastic expectations of the
Augustan age at the beginning of the Christian
Era, or of the changes in the spirit of the West
which accompanied the end of the first millen-
nium. Today, as the end of the second millen-
nium draws near, we are again living in an age
filled with apocalyptic images of universal de-

struction. What is the significance of that split, symbolized by the "Iron Curtain," which divides humanity into two halves? What will become of our civilization, and of man himself, if the hydrogen bombs begin to go off, or if the spiritual and moral darkness of State absolutism should spread over Europe?

We have no reason to take this threat lightly. Everywhere in the West there are subversive minorities who, sheltered by our humanitarianism and our sense of justice, hold the incendiary torches ready, with nothing to stop the spread of their ideas except the critical reason of a single, fairly intelligent, mentally stable stratum of the population. One should not, however, overestimate the thickness of this stratum. It varies from country to country in accordance with national temperament. Also, it is regionally dependent on public education and is subject to the influence of acutely disturbing factors of a political and economic nature. Taking plebiscites as a criterion, one could on an optimistic estimate put its upper limit at about 40 per cent of the electorate. A rather more pessimistic view would not be unjustified either, since the gift of reason and critical reflection is not one of man's outstanding peculiarities, and even where it exists it proves to be wavering and inconstant, the more so, as a rule, the bigger the political groups are. The mass crushes out the insight and reflection that are still possible with the individual, and this necessarily leads to doctrinaire and authoritarian tyranny if ever the constitutional State should succumb to a fit of weakness.

Rational argument can be conducted with some prospect of success only so long as the emotionality of a given situation does not exceed a certain critical degree. If the affective temperature rises above this level, the possibility of reason's having any effect ceases and its place is taken by slogans and chimerical wish-fantasies. That is to say, a sort of collective possession results which rapidly develops into a psychic epidemic. In this state all those elements whose existence is merely tolerated as asocial under the rule of reason come to the top. Such individuals are by no means rare curiosities to be met with only in prisons and lunatic asylums. For every manifest case of insanity there are, in my estimation, at least ten latent cases who seldom get to the point of breaking out openly but whose views and behavior, for all their appearance of normality, are influenced by unconsciously morbid and perverse factors. There are, of course, no medi-

cal statistics on the frequency of latent psychoses—for understandable reasons. But even
if their number should amount to less than ten
times that of the manifest psychoses and of
manifest criminality, the relatively small per-
centage of the population figures they represent is more than compensated for by the
peculiar dangerousness of these people. Their
mental state is that of a collectively excited
group ruled by affective judgments and wish-
fantasies. In a state of "collective possession"
they are the adapted ones and consequently
they feel quite at home in it. They know from
their own experience the language of these
conditions and they know how to handle them.
Their chimerical ideas, upborne by fanatical
resentment, appeal to the collective irrationality and find fruitful soil there, for they express
all those motives and resentments which lurk
in more normal people under the cloak of reason and insight. They are, therefore, despite
their small number in comparison with the
population as a whole, dangerous as sources of
infection precisely because the so-called normal person possesses only a limited degree of
self-knowledge.

Most people confuse "self-knowledge" with
knowledge of their conscious ego personalities.

Anyone who has ego-consciousness at all takes it for granted that he knows himself. But the ego knows only its own contents, not the unconscious and its contents. People measure their self-knowledge by what the average person in their social environment knows of himself, but not by the real psychic facts which are for the most part hidden from them. In this respect the psyche behaves like the body with its physiological and anatomical structure, of which the average person knows very little too. Although he lives in it and with it, most of it is totally unknown to the layman, and special scientific knowledge is needed to acquaint consciousness with what is known of the body, not to speak of all that is *not* known, which also exists.

What is commonly called "self-knowledge" is therefore a very limited knowledge, most of it dependent on social factors, of what goes on in the human psyche. Hence one is always coming up against the prejudice that such and such a thing does not happen "with us" or "in our family" or among our friends and acquaintances, and on the other hand, one meets with equally illusory assumptions about the alleged presence of qualities which merely serve to cover up the true facts of the case.

In this broad belt of unconsciousness, which is immune to conscious criticism and control, we stand defenseless, open to all kinds of influences and psychic infections. As with all dangers, we can guard against the risk of psychic infection only when we know what is attacking us, and how, where and when the attack will come. Since self-knowledge is a matter of getting to know the individual facts, theories help very little in this respect. For the more a theory lays claim to universal validity, the less capable it is of doing justice to the individual facts. Any theory based on experience is necessarily *statistical;* that is to say, it formulates an *ideal average* which abolishes all exceptions at either end of the scale and replaces them by an abstract mean. This mean is quite valid, though it need not necessarily occur in reality. Despite this it figures in the theory as an unassailable fundamental fact. The exceptions at either extreme, though equally factual, do not appear in the final result at all, since they cancel each other out. If, for instance, I determine the weight of each stone in a bed of pebbles and get an average weight of 145 grams, this tells me very little about the real nature of the pebbles. Anyone who thought, on the basis of these findings, that he could pick up a pebble of 145 grams at the first try would be in for a serious disappointment. Indeed, it might well happen that however long he searched he would not find a single pebble weighing exactly 145 grams.

The statistical method shows the facts in the light of the ideal average but does not give us a picture of their empirical reality. While reflecting an indisputable aspect of reality, it can falsify the actual truth in a most misleading way. This is particularly true of theories which are based on statistics. The distinctive thing about real facts, however, is their individuality. Not to put too fine a point on it, one could say that the real picture consists of nothing but exceptions to the rule, and that, in consequence, absolute reality has predominantly the character of *irregularity*.

These considerations must be borne in mind whenever there is talk of a theory serving as a guide to self-knowledge. There is and can be no self-knowledge based on theoretical assumptions, for the object of self-knowledge is an individual—a relative exception and an irregular phenomenon. Hence it is not the universal and the regular that characterize the individual, but rather the unique. He is not to be understood as a recurrent unit but as something unique and singular which in the last analysis can neither be known nor compared with anything else. At the same time man, as member of a species, can and must be described as a statistical unit; otherwise nothing general could be said about him. For this purpose he has to be regarded as a comparative unit. This results in a universally valid anthropology or psychology, as the case may be, with an abstract picture of man as an average unit from which all individual features have been removed. But it is precisely these features which are of paramount importance for *understanding* man. If I want to understand an individual human being, I must lay aside all scientific knowledge of the average man and discard all theories in order to adopt a completely new and unprejudiced attitude. I can only approach the task of *understanding* with a free and open mind, whereas *knowledge* of man, or insight into human character, presupposes all sorts of knowledge about mankind in general.

Now whether it is a question of understanding a fellow human being or of self-knowledge, I must in both cases leave all theoretical assumptions behind me. Since scientific knowledge not only enjoys universal esteem but, in the eyes of modern man, counts as the only intellectual and spiritual authority, understanding the individual obliges me to commit *lèse majesté,* so to speak, to turn a blind eye to scientific knowledge. This is a sacrifice not lightly made, for the scientific attitude cannot rid itself so easily of its sense of responsibility. And if the psychologist happens to be a doctor who wants not only to classify his patient scientifically but also to understand him as a human being, he is threatened with a conflict of duties between the two diametrically opposed and mutually exclusive attitudes of knowledge, on the one hand, and understanding, on the other. This conflict cannot be solved by an either-or but only by a kind of two-way thinking: doing one thing while not losing sight of the other.

In view of the fact that in principle, the positive advantages of *knowledge* work specifically to the disadvantage of *understanding,* the judgment resulting therefrom is likely to be something of a paradox. Judged scientifically, the individual is nothing but a unit which repeats itself ad infinitum and could just as well be designated with a letter of the alphabet. For understanding, on the other hand, it is just the unique individual human being who, when stripped of all those conformities and regularities so dear to the heart of the scientist, is the supreme and only real object of investigation. The doctor, above all, should be aware of this contradiction. On the one hand, he is equipped with the statistical truths of his scientific training, and on the other, he is faced with the task of treating a sick person who, especially in the case of psychic suffering, requires *individual understanding*. The more schematic the treatment is, the more resistances it—quite rightly —calls up in the patient, and the more the cure is jeopardized. The psychotherapist sees himself compelled, willy-nilly, to regard the individuality of a patient as an essential fact in the picture and to arrange his methods of treatment accordingly. Today, over the whole field of medicine, it is recognized that the task of the doctor consists in treating the sick person, not an abstract illness.

This illustration in the case of medicine is only a special instance of the problem of education and training in general. Scientific education is based in the main on statistical truths and abstract knowledge and therefore imparts an unrealistic, rational picture of the world, in which the individual, as a merely marginal phenomenon, plays no role. The individual, however, as an irrational datum, is the true and authentic carrier of reality, the *concrete* man as opposed to the unreal ideal or normal man to whom the scientific statements refer. What is more, most of the natural sciences try to represent the results of their investigations as though these had come into existence without man's intervention, in such a way that the collaboration of the psyche—an indispensable factor—remains invisible. (An exception to this is modern physics, which recognizes that the observed is not independent of the observer.) So in this respect, too, science conveys a picture of the world from which a real human psyche appears to be excluded—the very antithesis of the "humanities."

Under the influence of scientific assumptions, not only the psyche but the individual man and, indeed, all individual events whatsoever suffer a leveling down and a process of blurring that distorts the picture of reality into a conceptual average. We ought not to underestimate the psychological effect of the statistical world picture: it displaces the individual in favor of anonymous units that pile up into mass formations. Science supplies us with, instead of the concrete individual, the names of organizations and, at the highest point, the abstract idea of the State as the principle of political reality. The moral responsibility of the individual is then inevitably replaced by the policy of the State *(raison d'état)*. Instead of moral and mental differentiation of the individual, you have public welfare and the raising of the living standard. The goal and meaning of individual life (which is the only *real* life) no longer lie in individual development but in the policy of the State, which is thrust upon the individual from outside and consists in the execution of an abstract idea which ultimately tends to attract all life to itself. The individual is increasingly deprived of the moral decision as to how he should live his own life, and instead is ruled, fed, clothed and educated as a social unit, accommodated in the appropriate housing unit, and amused in accordance with the standards that give pleasure and satisfaction to the masses. The rulers, in their turn, are just as much social units as the ruled and are distinguished only by the fact that they are specialized mouthpieces of the State doctrine. They do not need to be personalities capable of judgment, but thoroughgoing specialists who are unusable outside their line of business. State policy decides what shall be taught and studied.

The seemingly omnipotent State doctrine is

for its part manipulated in the name of State policy by those occupying the highest positions in the government, where all the power is concentrated. Whoever, by election or caprice, gets into one of these positions is no longer subservient to authority, for he is the State policy itself and within the limits of the situation can proceed at his own discretion. With Louis XIV he can say, *"L'état c'est moi."* He is thus the only individual or, at any rate, one of the few individuals who could make use of their individuality if only they knew how to differentiate themselves from the State doctrine. They are more likely, however, to be the slaves of their own fictions. Such one-sidedness is always compensated psychologically by unconscious subversive tendencies. Slavery and rebellion are inseparable correlates. Hence, rivalry for power and exaggerated distrust pervade the entire organism from top to bottom. Furthermore, in order to compensate for its chaotic formlessness, a mass always produces a "Leader," who almost infallibly becomes the victim of his own inflated ego-consciousness, as numerous examples in history show.

This development becomes logically unavoidable the moment the individual masses together with others and becomes obsolete. Apart from agglomerations of huge masses of people, in which the individual disappears anyway, one of the chief factors responsible for psychological mass-mindedness is scientific rationalism, which robs the individual of his foundations and his dignity. As a social unit he has lost his individuality and become a mere abstract number in the bureau of statistics. He can only play the role of an interchangeable unit of infinitesimal importance. Looked at rationally and from outside, that is exactly what he is, and from this point of view it seems positively absurd to go on talking about the value or meaning of the individual. Indeed, one can hardly imagine how one ever came to endow individual human life with so much dignity when the truth to the contrary is as plain as the palm of your hand.

Seen from this standpoint, the individual really is of diminishing importance and anyone who wished to dispute this would soon find himself at a loss for arguments. The fact that the individual feels himself or the members of his family or the esteemed friends in his circle to be important merely underlines the slightly comic subjectivity of his feeling. For

what are the few compared with ten thousand
or a hundred thousand, let alone a million?
This recalls the argument of a thoughtful
friend with whom I once got caught up in a
huge crowd of people. Suddenly he exclaimed,
"Here you have the most convincing reason
for not believing in immortality: *all those people* want to be immortal!"

The bigger the crowd the more negligible
the individual becomes. But if the individual,
overwhelmed by the sense of his own puniness
and impotence, should feel that his life has
lost its meaning—which, after all, is not identical with public welfare and higher standards
of living—then he is already on the road to
State slavery and, without knowing or want-
ing it, has become its proselyte. The man who
looks only outside and quails before the big
battalions has no resource with which to com-
bat the evidence of his senses and his
reason. But that is just what is happening today: we are all fascinated and overawed by
statistical truths and large numbers and are
daily apprised of the nullity and futility of
the individual personality, since it is not represented and personified by any mass organization. Conversely, those personages who strut

about on the world stage and whose voices are heard far and wide seem, to the uncritical public, to be borne along on some mass movement or on the tide of public opinion and for this reason are either applauded or execrated. Since mass suggestion plays the predominant role here, it remains a moot point whether their message is their own, for which they are personally responsible, or whether they merely function as a megaphone for collective opinion.

Under these circumstances it is small wonder that individual judgment grows increasingly uncertain of itself and that responsibility is collectivized as much as possible, i.e., is shuffled off by the individual and delegated to a corporate body. In this way the individual becomes more and more a function of society, which in its turn usurps the function of the real life carrier, whereas, in actual fact, society is nothing more than an abstract idea like the State. Both are hypostatized, that is, have become autonomous. The State in particular is turned into a quasi-animate personality from whom everything is expected. In reality it is only a camouflage for those individuals who know how to manipulate it. Thus the constitutional State drifts into the situation of a primitive form of society, namely the communism of a primitive tribe where everybody is subject to the autocratic rule of a chief or an oligarchy.

# II

## RELIGION AS THE COUNTERBALANCE TO MASS-MINDEDNESS

IN ORDER TO FREE THE FICTION OF THE SOVereign State—in other words, the whims of those who manipulate it—from every wholesome restriction, all socio-political movements tending in this direction invariably try to cut the ground from under the *religions*. For, in order to turn the individual into a function of the State, his dependence on anything beside the State must be taken from him. But religion means dependence on and submission to the irrational facts of experience. These do not refer directly to social and physical conditions; they concern far more the individual's psychic attitude.

But it is possible to have an attitude to the external conditions of life only when there is a point of reference outside them. The religions give, or claim to give, such a standpoint, thereby enabling the individual to exercise his judgment and his power of decision. They build up a reserve, as it were, against the obvious and inevitable force of circumstances to which everyone is exposed who lives only in the outer world and has no other ground under his feet except the pavement. If statistical reality is the only reality, then it is the sole authority. There is then only *one* condition, and since no contrary condition exists, judgment and decision are not only superfluous but impossible. Then the individual is bound to be a function of statistics and hence a function of the State or whatever the abstract principle of order may be called.

The religions, however, teach another authority opposed to that of the "world." The doctrine of the individual's dependence on God makes just as high a claim upon him as the world does. It may even happen that the absoluteness of this claim estranges him from the world in the same way he is estranged from himself when he succumbs to the collective mentality. He can forfeit his judgment and power of decision in the former case (for the sake of religious doctrine) quite as much as in the latter. This is the goal the religions openly aspire to unless they compromise with the State. When they do, I prefer to call them not "religions" but "creeds." A creed gives expression to a definite collective belief, whereas the word *religion* expresses a subjective relationship to certain metaphysical, extramundane factors. A creed is a confession of faith intended chiefly for the world at large and is thus an intramundane affair, while the meaning and purpose of religion lie in the relationship of the individual to God (Christianity, Judaism, Islam) or to the path of salvation and liberation (Buddhism). From this basic fact all ethics is derived, which without the individual's responsibility before God can be called nothing more than conventional morality.

Since they are compromises with mundane reality, the creeds have accordingly seen themselves obliged to undertake a progressive codification of their views, doctrines and customs and in so doing have externalized themselves to such an extent that the authentic religious element in them—the living relationship to and direct confrontation with their extramundane point of reference—has been thrust into the background. The denominational standpoint measures the worth and importance of the subjective religious relationship by the yardstick of traditional doctrine, and where this is not so frequent, as in Protestantism, one immediately hears talk of pietism, sectarianism, eccentricity, and so forth, as soon as anyone claims to be guided by God's will. A creed coincides with the established Church or, at any rate, forms a public institution whose members include not only true believers but vast numbers of people who can only be described as "indifferent" in matters of religion and who belong to it simply by force of habit. Here the difference between a creed and a religion becomes palpable.

To be the adherent of a creed, therefore, is not always a religious matter but more often a social one and, as such, it does nothing to give the individual any foundation. For support he has to depend exclusively on his relation to an authority which is not of this world. The criterion here is not lip service to a creed but the psychological fact that the life of the individual is not determined solely by the ego and its opinions or by social factors, but quite as much, if not more, by a transcendent authority. It is not ethical principles, however lofty, or creeds, however orthodox, that lay the foundations for the freedom and autonomy of the individual, but simply and solely the empirical awareness, the incontrovertible experience of an intensely personal, reciprocal relationship between man and an extramundane authority which acts as a counterpoise to the "world" and its "reason."

This formulation will not please either the mass man or the collective believer. For the former the policy of the State is the supreme principle of thought and action. Indeed, this was the purpose for which he was enlightened, and accordingly the mass man grants the individual a right to exist only in so far as the individual is a function of the State. The believer, on the other hand, while admitting that the State has a moral and factual claim, confesses to the belief that not only man but the State that rules him is subject to the overlordship of "God" and that, in case of doubt, the supreme decision will be made by God and not by the State. Since I do not presume to any metaphysical judgments, I must leave it an open question whether the "world," i.e., the phenomenal world of man, and hence nature in general, is the "opposite" of God or not. I can only point to the fact that the psychological opposition between these two realms of experience is not only vouched for in the New Testament but is still exemplified very plainly today in the negative attitude of the dictator States to religion, and of the Church to atheism and materialism.

Just as man, as a social being, cannot in the long run exist without a tie to the community, so the individual will never find the real justification for his existence, and his own spiritual and moral autonomy, anywhere except in an extramundane principle capable of relativizing the overpowering influence of external factors. The individual who is not anchored in God can offer no resistance on his own resources to the physical and moral blandishments of the world. For this he needs the evidence of inner, transcendent experience which alone can protect him from the otherwise inevitable submersion in the mass. Merely intellectual or even moral insight into the stultification and moral irresponsibility of the mass man is a negative recognition only and amounts to not much more than a wavering on the road to the atomization of the individual. It lacks the driving force of religious conviction, since it is merely rational. The dictator State has one great advantage over bourgeois reason: along with the individual it swallows up his religious forces. The State has taken the place of God; that is why, seen from this angle, the socialist dictatorships are religions and State slavery is a form of worship. But the religious function cannot be dislocated and falsified in this way without giving rise to secret doubts, which are immediately repressed so as to avoid conflict with the prevailing trends towards mass-mindedness. The result, as always in such cases, is overcompensation in the form of *fanaticism,* which in its turn is used as a weapon for stamping out the least flicker of opposition. Free opinion is stifled and moral decision ruthlessly suppressed, on the plea that the end justifies the means, even the vilest. The policy of the State is exalted to a creed, the leader or party boss becomes a demigod beyond good and evil, and his votaries are honored as heroes, martyrs, apostles, missionaries. There is only *one* truth and beside it no other. It is sacrosanct and above criticism. Anyone who thinks differently is a heretic, who, as we know from history, is threatened with all manner of unpleasant things. Only the party boss, who holds the political power in his hands, can interpret the State doctrine authentically, and he does so just as suits him.

When, through mass rule, the individual becomes social unit No. so-and-so and the State is elevated to the supreme principle, it is only to be expected that the religious function too will be sucked into the maelstrom. Religion, as the careful observation and taking account of certain invisible and uncontrollable factors, is an *instinctive attitude* peculiar to man, and its manifestations can be followed all through human history. Its evident purpose is to maintain the psychic balance, for the natural man has an equally natural "knowledge" of the fact that his conscious functions may at any time be thwarted by uncontrollable happenings coming from inside as well as from outside. For this reason he has always taken care that any difficult decision likely to have consequences for himself and others shall be rendered safe by suitable measures of a religious nature. Offerings are made to the invisible powers, formidable blessings are pronounced, and all kinds of solemn rites are performed. Everywhere and at all times there have been *rites d'entrée et de sortie* whose magical efficacy is denied and which are impugned as magic and superstition by rationalists incapable of psychological insight. But magic has above all a psychological effect whose importance should not be underestimated. The performance of a "magical" action gives the person concerned a feeling of security which is absolutely essential for carrying out a decision, because a decision is inevitably somewhat one-sided and is therefore rightly felt to be a risk. Even a dictator thinks it necessary not only to accompany his acts of State with threats but to stage them with all manner of solemnities. Brass bands, flags, banners, parades and monster demonstrations are no different in principle from ecclesiastical processions, cannonades and fireworks to scare off demons. Only, the suggestive parade of State power engenders a collective feeling of security which, unlike religious demonstrations, gives the individual no protection against his inner demonism. Hence he will cling all the more to the power of the State, i.e., to the mass, thus delivering himself up to it psychically as well as morally and putting the finishing touch to his social depotentiation. The State, like the Church, demands enthusiasm, self-sacrifice and love, and if religion requires or presupposes the "fear of God," then the dictator State takes good care to provide the necessary terror.

When the rationalist directs the main force of his attack against the magical effect of the rite as asserted by tradition, he has in reality completely missed the mark. The essential point, the *psychological* effect, is overlooked, although both parties make use of it for directly opposite purposes. A similar situation prevails with regard to their respective conceptions of the goal. The goals of religion—deliverance from evil, reconciliation with God, rewards in the hereafter, and so on—turn into worldly promises about freedom from care for one's daily bread, the just distribution of material goods, universal prosperity in the future, and shorter working hours. That the fulfillment of these promises is as far off as Paradise only furnishes yet another analogy and underlines the fact that the masses have been converted from an extramundane goal to a purely worldly belief, which is extolled with exactly the same religious fervor and exclusiveness that the creeds display in the other direction.

In order not to repeat myself unnecessarily, I shall not enumerate all the parallels between worldly and otherworldly beliefs, but shall content myself with emphasizing the fact that a natural function which has existed from the beginning, like the religious function, cannot be disposed of with rationalistic and so-called enlightened criticism. You can, of course, represent the doctrinal contents of the creeds as impossible and subject them to ridicule, but such methods miss the point and do not hit the religious function which forms the basis of the creeds. Religion, in the sense of conscientious regard for the irrational factors of the psyche and individual fate, reappears—evilly distorted—in the deification of the State and the dictator: *Naturam expellas furca tamen usque recurret* (you can throw out Nature with a pitchfork, but she'll always turn up again). The leaders and dictators, having weighed up the situation correctly, are therefore doing their best to gloss over the all too obvious parallel with the deification of Caesar and to hide their real power behind the fiction of the State, though this, of course, alters nothing.*

As I have already pointed out, the dictator State, besides robbing the individual of his rights, has also cut the ground from under his feet psychically by depriving him of the metaphysical foundations of his existence. The ethical decision of the individual human being no longer counts—what alone matters is the blind movement of the masses, and the lie has thus

* Since this essay was written, in the spring of 1956, there has been a noticeable reaction in the U.S.S.R. to this objectionable state of affairs.

become the operative principle of political action. The State has drawn the logical conclusions from this, as the existence of many millions of State slaves completely deprived of all rights mutely testifies.

Both the dictator State and denominational religion lay quite particular emphasis on the idea of *community*. This is the basic ideal of "communism," and it is thrust down the throats of the people so much that it has the exact opposite of the desired effect: it inspires divisive mistrust. The Church, which is no less emphasized, appears on the other side as a communal ideal, and where the Church is notoriously weak, as in Protestantism, the hope of or belief in a "communal experience" makes up for the painful lack of cohesion. As can easily be seen, "community" is an indispensable aid in the organization of masses and is therefore a two-edged weapon. Just as the addition of however many zeroes will never make a unit, so the value of a community depends on the spiritual and moral stature of the individuals composing it. For this reason one cannot expect from the community any effect that would outweigh the suggestive influence of the environment—that is, a real and fundamental change in individuals, whether for good or for bad. Such changes can come only from the personal encounter between man and man, but not from communistic or Christian baptisms en masse, which do not touch the inner man. How superficial the effect of communal propaganda actually is can be seen from recent events in Eastern Europe.* The communal ideal reckons without its host, overlooking the individual human being, who in the end will assert his claims.

* Added in January 1957.

# THE POSITION OF THE WEST
# ON THE QUESTION OF RELIGION

CONFRONTING THIS DEVELOPMENT IN THE twentieth century of our Christian Era, the Western world stands with its heritage of Roman law, the treasures of Judaeo-Christian ethics grounded on metaphysics, and its ideal of the inalienable rights of man. Anxiously it asks itself the question: How can this development be brought to a standstill or put into reverse? It is useless to pillory the socialist dictatorship as utopian and to condemn its economic principles as unreasonable, because, in the first place, the criticizing West has only itself to talk to, its arguments being heard only on this side of the Iron Curtain, and, in the second place, any economic principles you like can be put into practice so long as you are

43

prepared to accept the sacrifices they entail. You can carry through any social and economic reforms you please if, like Stalin, you let three million peasants starve to death and have a few million unpaid laborers at your disposal. A State of this kind has no social or economic crises to fear. So long as its power is intact—that is to say, so long as there is a well-disciplined and well-fed police army in the offing—it can maintain its existence for an indefinitely long period and can go on increasing its power to an indefinite extent. In accordance with its excess birth rate, it can raise the number of its unpaid workers almost at will in order to compete with its rivals, regardless of the world market, which is to a large measure dependent on wages. A real danger can come to it only from outside, through the threat of military attack. But this risk grows less every year, firstly because the war potential of the dictator States is steadily increasing, and secondly because the West cannot afford to arouse latent Russian or Chinese nationalism and chauvinism by an attack which would divert their well-meant undertakings into a hopelessly wrong channel.

So far as one can see, only one possibility remains, and that is a breakdown of power

from within, which must, however, be left to
follow its own inner development. Any support from outside at present would have little
effect, in view of the existing security measures and the danger of nationalistic reactions.
The absolute State has an army of fanatical
missionaries to do its bidding in matters of
foreign policy, and these in their turn can count
on a fifth column who are guaranteed asylum
under the laws and constitution of the Western
States. In addition the communes of believers,
very strong in places, considerably weaken
Western governments' powers of decision,
whereas the West has no opportunity to exert
a similar influence on our rivals, though we
are probably not wrong in surmising that
there is a certain amount of opposition among
the masses in the East. There are always up-
right and truth-loving people to whom lying
and tyranny are hateful, but one cannot judge
whether they exert any decisive influence on
the masses under the police regimes.*

In view of this uncomfortable situation the
question is heard again and again in the West:
What can we do to counter this threat from
the East? Even though the West has consid-

* Recent events in Poland and Hungary have shown that
this opposition is more considerable than could have been
foreseen.

erable industrial power and a sizable defense potential at its command, we cannot rest content with this, for we know that even the biggest guns and the heaviest industry with its relatively high living standard are not enough to check the psychic infection spread by religious fanaticism.

The West has unfortunately not yet awakened to the fact that our appeal to idealism and reason and other desirable virtues, delivered with so much enthusiasm, is mere sound and fury. It is a puff of wind swept away in the storm of religious faith, however twisted this faith may appear to us. We are faced, not with a situation that can be overcome by rational or moral arguments, but with an unleashing of emotional forces and ideas engendered by the spirit of the times, and these, as we know from experience, are not much influenced by rational reflection and still less by moral exhortation. It has been correctly realized in many quarters that the alexipharmic, the antidote, should in this case be an equally potent faith of a different and nonmaterialistic kind, and that the religious attitude grounded upon it would be the only effective defense against the danger of psychic infection. Unhappily, the little word "should," which never fails to appear in this connection, points to a certain weakness, if not the absence, of this desideratum. Not only does the West lack a uniform faith that could block the progress of a fanatical ideology, but, as the father of Marxist philosophy, it makes use of exactly the same spiritual assumptions, the same arguments and aims. Although the Churches in the West enjoy full freedom, they are not less full or empty than in the East. Yet they exercise no noticeable influence on the broad course of politics. The disadvantage of a creed as a public institution is that it serves two masters: on the one hand, it derives its existence from the relationship of man to God, and on the other hand, it owes a duty to the State, i.e., to the world, in which connection it can appeal to the saying "Render unto Caesar . . ." and various other admonitions in the New Testament. In early times and until comparatively recently there was, therefore, talk of "powers ordained by God" (Romans 13:1). Today this conception is antiquated. The Churches stand for traditional and collective convictions which in the case of many of their adherents are no longer based on their own inner experience but on *unreflecting belief,* which is notoriously apt to disappear as soon as one begins thinking about it. The content of belief then comes into collision with knowledge, and it often turns out that the irrationality of the former is no match for the ratiocinations of the latter. Belief is no adequate substitute for inner experience, and where this is absent even a strong faith which came miraculously as a gift of grace may depart equally miraculously. People call faith the true religious experience, but they do not stop to think that actually it is a secondary phenomenon arising from the fact that something happened to us in the first place which instilled πίστις into us—that is, trust and loyalty. This experience has a definite content that can be interpreted in terms of one or other of the denominational creeds. But the more this is so, the more the possibilities of these conflicts with knowledge mount up, which in themselves are quite pointless. That is to say, the standpoint of the creeds is archaic; they are full of impressive mythological symbolism which, if taken literally, comes into insufferable conflict with knowledge. But if, for instance, the statement that Christ rose from the dead is to be understood not literally but symbolically, then it is capable of various interpretations that do not collide with knowledge and do not impair the meaning of the statement.

The objection that understanding it symbolically puts an end to the Christian's hope of immortality is invalid, because long before the coming of Christianity mankind believed in a life after death and therefore had no need of the Easter event as a guarantee of immortality. The danger that a mythology understood too literally, and as taught by the Church, will suddenly be repudiated lock, stock and barrel is today greater than ever. Is it not time that the Christian mythology, instead of being wiped out, was understood symbolically for once?

It is still too early to say what might be the consequences of a general recognition of the fatal parallelism between the State religion of the Marxists and the State religion of the Church. The absolutist claim of a *Civitas Dei* represented by man bears an unfortunate resemblance to the "divinity" of the State, and the moral conclusion drawn by Ignatius Loyola from the authority of the Church ("the end sanctifies the means") anticipates the lie as a political instrument in an exceedingly dangerous way. Both demand unqualified submission to faith and thus curtail man's freedom, the one his freedom before God and the other his freedom before the State, thereby digging the grave for the individual. The fragile existence of the individual, the unique carrier of life, is threatened on both sides, despite their respective promises of spiritual and material idylls to come—and how many of us can in the long run fight against the proverbial wisdom of "a bird in the hand is worth two in the bush"? Besides which, the West cherishes the same "scientific" and rationalistic *Weltanschauung* with its statistical leveling-down tendency and materialistic aims as the State religion of the Eastern bloc, as I have explained above.

What, then, has the West, with its political and denominational schisms, to offer to modern man in his need? Nothing, unfortunately, except a variety of paths all leading to one goal which is practically indistinguishable from the Marxist ideal. It requires no special effort of understanding to see where the Communist ideology gets the certainty of its belief that time is on its side, and that the world is ripe for conversion. The facts speak a language that is all too plain in this respect. It will not help us in the West to shut our eyes to this and not recognize our fatal vulnerability. Anyone who has once learned to submit absolutely to a collective belief and to renounce his eternal right to freedom and the equally eternal duty of individual responsibility will persist in this attitude, and will be able to set out with the same credulity and the same lack of criticism in the reverse direction, if another and manifestly "better" belief is foisted upon his alleged idealism. What happened not so long ago to a civilized European nation? We accuse the Germans of having forgotten it all again already, but the truth is that we don't know for certain whether something similar might not happen elsewhere. It would not be surprising if it did and if another civilized nation succumbed to the infection of a uniform and one-sided idea. America, which—*O quae mutatio rerum!*—forms the real political backbone of Western Europe, seems to be immune because of the outspoken counterposition she has adopted, but in point of fact she is perhaps even more vulnerable than Europe, since her educational system is the most influenced by the scientific *Weltanschauung* with its statistical truths, and her mixed population finds it difficult to strike roots in a soil that is practically without history. The historical and humanistic type of education so sorely needed in such circumstances leads, on the contrary, a Cinderella existence. Though Europe possesses this latter requirement, she uses it to her own undoing in the form of nation-alistic egoisms and paralyzing skepticism. Common to both is the materialistic and collectivist goal, and both lack the very thing that expresses and grips the whole man, namely, an idea which puts the individual human being in the center as the measure of all things.

This idea alone is enough to arouse the most violent doubts and resistances on all sides, and one could almost go so far as to assert that the valuelessness of the individual in comparison with large numbers is the one belief that meets with universal and unanimous assent. To be sure, we all say that this is the century of the common man, that he is the lord of the earth, the air and the water, and that on his decision hangs the historical fate of the nations. This proud picture of human grandeur is unfortunately an illusion only and is counterbalanced by a reality which is very different. In this reality man is the slave and victim of the machines that have conquered space and time for him; he is intimidated and endangered by the might of the war technique which is supposed to safeguard his physical existence; his spiritual and moral freedom, though guaranteed within limits in one half of his world, is threatened with chaotic disorientation, and in the other half it is abolished altogether. Finally, to add comedy to tragedy, this lord of the elements, this universal arbiter, hugs to his bosom notions which stamp his dignity as worthless and turn his autonomy into an absurdity. All his achievements and possessions do not make him bigger; on the contrary, they diminish him, as the fate of the factory worker under the rule of a "just" distribution of goods clearly demonstrates.

# IV

## THE INDIVIDUAL'S UNDERSTANDING OF HIMSELF

IT IS ASTOUNDING THAT MAN, THE INSTIGATOR, inventor and vehicle of all these developments, the originator of all judgments and decisions and the planner of the future, must make himself such a *quantité négligeable*. The contradiction, the paradoxical evaluation of humanity by man himself, is in truth a matter for wonder, and one can only explain it as springing from an extraordinary uncertainty of judgment—in other words, man is an enigma to himself. This is understandable, seeing that he lacks the means of comparison necessary for self-knowledge. He knows how to distinguish himself from the other animals in point of anatomy and phsysiology, but as a conscious, reflecting being, gifted with speech, he lacks all criteria for self-judgment. He is on this planet a unique phenomenon which he cannot compare with anything else. The possibility of comparison and hence of self-knowledge would arise only if he could establish relations with quasi-human mammals inhabiting other stars.

Until then man must continue to resemble a hermit who knows that in respect of comparative anatomy he has affinities with the anthropoids but, to judge by appearances, is extraordinarily different from his cousins in respect of his psyche. It is just in this most important characteristic of his species that he cannot know himself and therefore remains a mystery to himself. The differences of degree within his own species are of little significance compared with the possibilities of self-knowledge which would be occasioned by an encounter with a creature of similar structure but different origin. Our psyche, which is primarily responsible for all the historical changes wrought by the hand of man on the face of this planet, remains an insoluble puzzle and an incomprehensible wonder, an object of abiding perplexity—a feature it shares with all Nature's secrets. In regard to the latter we still have hope of making more discoveries and finding answers to the most difficult questions. But in regard to the psyche and psychology there seems to be a curious hesitancy. Not only is it the youngest of the empirical sciences, but it has great difficulty in getting anywhere near its proper object.

In the same way that our misconception of the solar system had to be freed from prejudice by Copernicus, the most strenuous efforts of a well-nigh revolutionary nature were needed to free psychology, first from the spell of mythological ideas, and then from the prejudice that the psyche is, on the one hand, a mere epiphenomenon of a biochemical process in the brain or, on the other hand, a wholly unapproachable and recondite matter. The connection with the brain does not in itself prove that the psyche is an epiphenomenon, a secondary function casually dependent on biochemical processes. Nevertheless, we know only too well how much the psychic function can be disturbed by verifiable processes in the brain, and this fact is so impressive that the subsidiary nature of the psyche seems an almost unavoidable inference. The phenomena of parapsychology, however, warn us to be careful, for they point to a relativization of space and time through psychic factors which casts doubt on our naive and overhasty explanation of the parallels between the psychic and the physical. For the sake of this explanation people deny the findings of parapsychology outright, either for philosophical reasons or from intellectual laziness. This can hardly be considered a scientifically responsible attitude, even though it is a popular way out of a quite extraordinary intellectual difficulty. To assess the psychic phenomenon, we have to take account of all the other phenomena that come with it, and accordingly we can no longer practice any psychology that ignores the existence of the unconscious or of parapsychology.

The structure and physiology of the brain furnish no explanation of the psychic process. The psyche has a peculiar nature which cannot be reduced to anything else. Like physiology, it represents a relatively self-contained field of experience to which we must attribute a quite special importance because it holds within itself one of the two indispensable conditions for existence as such, namely, the phenomenon of consciousness. Without consciousness there would, practically speaking, be no world, for the world exists as such only in so far as it is consciously reflected and consciously expressed by a psyche. *Consciousness is a precondition of being.* Thus the psyche is endowed with the dignity of a cosmic principle, which philosophically and in fact gives it a position coequal with the principle of physical being. The carrier of this consciousness is the individual, who does not produce the psyche on his own volition but is, on the contrary, preformed by it and nourished by the gradual awakening of consciousness during childhood. If the psyche must be granted an overriding empirical importance, so also must the individual, who is the only immediate manifestation of the psyche.

This fact must be expressly emphasized for two reasons. Firstly, the individual psyche, just because of its individuality, is an exception to the statistical rule and is therefore robbed of one of its main characteristics when subjected to the leveling influence of statistical evaluation. Secondly, the Churches grant it validity only in so far as it acknowledges their dogmas —in other words, when it surrenders to a collective category. In both cases the will to individuality is regarded as egotistic obstinacy. Science devalues it as subjectivism, and the Churches condemn it morally as heresy and spiritual pride. As to the latter charge, it should not be forgotten that, unlike other religions,

Christianity holds at its core a symbol which has for its content the individual way of life of a man, the Son of Man, and that it even regards this individuation process as the incarnation and revelation of God himself. Hence the development of the self acquires a significance whose full implications have hardly begun to be appreciated, because too much attention to externals blocks the way to immediate inner experience. Were not the autonomy of the individual the secret longing of many people, this hard-pressed phenomenon would scarcely be able to survive the collective suppression either morally or spiritually.

All these obstacles make it more difficult to arrive at a correct appreciation of the human psyche, but they count for very little beside one other remarkable fact that deserves mentioning. This is the common psychiatric experience that the devaluation of the psyche and other resistances to psychological enlightenment are based in large measure on fear—on panic fear of the discoveries that might be made in the realm of the unconscious. These fears are found not only among persons who are frightened by the picture Freud painted of the unconscious; they also troubled the originator of psychoanalysis himself, who confessed to me that it was necessary to make a dogma of his sexual theory because this was the sole bulwark of reason against a possible "outburst of the black flood of occultism." In these words Freud was expressing his conviction that the unconscious still harbored many thing that might lend themselves to "occult" interpretations, as is in fact the case. These "archaic vestiges," or archetypal forms grounded on the instincts and giving expression to them, have a numinous quality that sometimes arouses fear. They are ineradicable, for they represent the ultimate foundations of the psyche itself. They cannot be grasped intellectually, and when one has destroyed one manifestation of them, they reappear in altered form. It is this fear of the unconscious psyche which not only impedes self-knowledge but is the gravest obstacle to a wider understanding and knowledge of psychology. Often the fear is so great that one dares not admit it even to oneself. Here is a question that every religious person should consider very seriously; he might get an illuminating answer.

A scientifically oriented psychology is bound to proceed abstractly; that is, it removes itself just sufficiently far from its object not to lose sight of it altogether. That is why the findings of laboratory psychology are, for all practical purposes, often so remarkably unenlightening and devoid of interest. The more the individual object dominates the field of vision, the more practical, detailed and alive will be the knowledge derived from it. This means that the objects of investigation, too, become more and more complicated and the uncertainty of individual factors increases proportionally to their number, thus increasing the possibility of error. Understandably enough, academic psychology is scared of this risk and prefers to avoid complex impunity. It has full freedom in the choice of questions it will put to Nature.

Medical psychology is very far from being in this more or less enviable position. Here the object puts the question and not the experimenter. The doctor is confronted with facts which are not of his choosing and which he probably never would choose if he were a free agent. It is the sickness or the patient that puts the crucial questions—in other words, Nature experiments with the doctor in expecting an answer from him. The uniqueness of the individual and of his situation stares the doctor in the face and demands an answer. His duty as a physician forces him to cope with a situation swarming with uncertainty factors. At first he will apply principles based on general experience, but he will soon realize that principles of this kind do not adequately express the facts and fail to meet the nature of the case. The deeper his understanding penetrates, the more the general principles lose their meaning. But these principles are the foundation of objective knowledge and the yardstick by which it is measured. With the growth of what both patient and doctor feel to be "understanding," the situation becomes increasingly subjectivized. What was an advantage to begin with threatens to turn into a dangerous disadvantage. Subjectivation (in technical terms, transference and countertransference) creates isolation from the environment, a social limitation which neither party wishes for but which invariably sets in when understanding predominates and is no longer balanced by knowledge. As understanding deepens, the further removed it becomes from knowledge. An ideal understanding would ultimately result in each party's unthinkingly going along with the other's experience—a state of uncritical passivity coupled with the most complete subjectivity and lack of social responsibility. Understanding carried to such lengths is in any case impossible, for it would require the virtual identification of two different individuals. Sooner or later the relationship reaches a point where one partner feels he is being forced to sacrifice his own individuality so that it may be assimilated by that of the other. This inevitable consequence breaks the understanding, for understanding presupposes the integral preservation of the individuality of both partners. It is therefore advisable to carry understanding only to the point where the balance between understanding and knowledge is reached, for understanding at all costs is injurious to both partners.

This problem arises whenever complex, individual situations have to be known and understood. It is the specific task of psychology to provide just this knowledge and understanding. It would also be the task of the confessor zealous in the cure of souls, were it not that his office inevitably obliges him to apply the yardstick of his denominational bias at the critical moment. As a result, the individual's right to exist as such is cut short by a collective prejudice and often curtailed in the most sensitive area. The only time this does not happen is when the religious symbol, for instance the model life of Christ, is understood correctly and felt by the indivdual to be adequate. How far this is the case today I would prefer to leave to the judgment of others. At all events, the doctor very often has to treat patients to whom denominational limitations mean little or nothing. His profession therefore compels him to have as few preconception as possible. Similarly, while respecting metaphysical (i.e, nonverifiable) convictions and assertions, he will take care not to credit them with universal validity. This caution is called for because individual traits of personality ought not to be twisted out of shape by arbitrary interventions from outside. The doctor must leave this to environmental influences, to the person's own inner development, and—in the widest sense—to fate with its wise or unwise decrees.

Many people will perhaps find this heightened caution exaggerated. In view of the fact, however, that there is in any case such a multitude of reciprocal influences at work in the dialectical process between two individuals, even if this process is conducted with the most tactful reserve, the responsible doctor will refrain from adding unnecessarily to the collective factors to which his patient has already succumbed. Moreover, he knows very well that the preaching of even the worthiest precepts only provokes the patient into open hostility or a secret resistance and thus needlessly endangers the aim of the treatment. The psychic situation of the individual is so menaced nowadays by advertisement, propaganda and other more or less well-meant advice and suggestions that for once in his life the patient might be offered a relationship that does not repeat the nauseating "you should," "you must" and similar confessions of impotence. Against the onslaught from outside no less than against its repercussions in the psyche of the individual the doctor sees himself obliged to play the role of counsel for the defense. Fear that anarchic instincts will thereby be let loose is a possibility that is greatly exaggerated, seeing that obvious safeguards exist within and without. Above all, there is the natural cowardice of most men to be reckoned with, not to mention morality, good taste and—last but not least—the penal code. This fear is nothing compared with the enormous effort it usually costs people to help the first stirrings of individuality into consciousness, let alone put them into effect. And where these individual impulses have broken through too impetuously and unthinkingly, the doctor must protect them from the patient's own clumsy recourse to shortsightedness, ruthlessness and cynicism.

As the dialectical discussion proceeds, a point

is reached where an evaluation of these individual impulses becomes necessary. By that time the patient should have acquired enough certainty of judgment to enable him to act on his own insight and decision and not from the mere wish to copy convention—even if he happens to agree with collective opinion. Unless he stands firmly on his own feet, the so-called objective values profit him nothing, since they then only serve as a substitute for character and so help to suppress his individuality. Naturally, society has an indisputable right to protect itself against arrant subjectivisms, but, in so far as society itself is composed of de-individualized persons, it is completely at the mercy of ruthless individualists. Let it band together into groups and organizations as much as it likes—it is just this banding together and the resultant extinction of the individual personality that makes it succumb so readily to a dictator. A million zeros joined together do not, unfortunately, add up to one. Ultimately everything depends on the quality of the individual, but the fatally shortsighted habit of our age is to think only in terms of large numbers and mass organizations, though one would think that the world had seen more than enough of what a well-disciplined mob can do in the hands of a single madman. Unfortunately, this realization does not seem to have penetrated very far—and our blindness in this respect is extremely dangerous. People go on blithely organizing and believing in the sovereign remedy of mass action, without the least consciousness of the fact that the most powerful organizations can be maintained only by the greatest ruthlessness of their leaders and the cheapest of slogans.

Curiously enough, the Churches too want to avail themselves of mass action in order to cast out the devil with Beelzebub—the very Churches whose care is the salvation of the *individual* soul. They too do not appear to have heard anything of the elementary axiom of mass psychology, that the individual becomes morally and spiritually inferior in the mass, and for this reason they do not burden themselves overmuch with their real task of helping the individual to achieve a *metanoia,* or rebirth of the spirit—*deo concedente.* It is, unfortunately, only too clear that if the individual is not truly regenerated in spirit, society cannot be either, for society is the sum total of individuals in need of redemption. I can therefore see it only as a delusion when the Churches try —as they apparently do—to rope the individual into a social organization and reduce him to a condition of diminished responsibility, instead of raising him out of the torpid, mindless mass and making clear to him that he is the one important factor and that the salvation of the world consists in the salvation of the individual soul. It is true that mass meetings parade such ideas before him and seek to impress them on him by dint of mass suggestion, with the unedifying result that when the intoxication has worn off, the mass man promptly succumbs to another even more obvious and still louder slogan. His individual relation to God would be an effective shield against these pernicious influences. Did Christ ever call his disciples to him at a mass meeting? Did the feeding of the five thousand bring him any followers who did not afterwards cry "Crucify him!" with the rest, when even the rock named Peter showed signs of wavering? And are not Jesus and Paul prototypes of those who, trusting their inner experience, have gone their own individual ways, disregarding public opinion?

This argument should certainly not cause us to overlook the reality of the situation confronting the Church. When the Church tries to give shape to the amorphous mass by uniting individuals into a community of believers with the help of suggestion and tries to hold such an

organization together, it is not only performing a great *social* service, but it also secures for
the individual the inestimable boon of a meaningful life form. These, however, are gifts which
as a rule confirm certain tendencies and do not
change them. As experience unfortunately
shows, the inner man remains unchanged however much community he has. His environment
cannot give him as a gift that which he can
win for himself only with effort and suffering.
On the contrary, a favorable environment
merely strengthens the dangerous tendency to
expect everything to originate from outside—
even that metamorphosis which external reality
cannot provide, namely, a deep-seated change
of the inner man, which is all the more urgent
in view of the mass phenomena of today and
the still greater problems of the increase of
population looming up in the future. It is
time we asked ourselves exactly what we are
lumping together in mass organizations and
what constitutes the nature of the individual
human being, i.e., of the real man and not the
statistical man. This is hardly possible except
through a new process of self-nourishment.

All mass movements, as one might expect,
slip with the greatest ease down an inclined
plane represented by large numbers. Where

the many are, there is security; what the many believe must of course be true; what the many want must be worth striving for, and necessary, and therefore good. In the clamor of the many there lies the power to snatch wish-fulfillments by force; sweetest of all, however, is that gentle and painless slipping back into the kingdom of childhood, into the paradise of parental care, into happy-go-luckiness and irresponsibility. All the thinking and looking after are done from the top; to all questions there is an answer; and for all needs the necessary provision is made. The infantile dream state of the mass man is so unrealistic that he never thinks to ask who is paying for this paradise. The balancing of accounts is left to a higher political or social authority, which welcomes the task, for its power is thereby increased; and the more power it has, the weaker and more helpless the individual becomes.

Wherever social conditions of this type develop on a large scale the road to tyranny lies open and the freedom of the individual turns into spiritual and physical slavery. Since every tyranny is *ipso facto* immoral and ruthless, it has much more freedom in the choice of its methods than an institution which still takes account of the individual. Should such an institution come into conflict with the organized State, it is soon made aware of the very real disadvantage of its morality and therefore feels compelled to avail itself of the same methods as its opponent. In this way the evil spreads almost of necessity, even when direct infection might be avoided. The danger of infection is greater where decisive importance is attached to large numbers and statistical values, as is everywhere the case in our Western world. The suffocating power of the masses is paraded before our eyes in one form or another every day in the newspapers, and the insignificance of the individual is rubbed into him so thoroughly that he loses all hope of making himself heard. The outworn ideals of *liberté, égalité, fraternité* help him not at all, as he can direct this appeal only to his executioners, the spokesmen of the masses.

 *Resistance to the organized mass can be effected only by the man who is as well organized in his individuality as the mass itself.* I fully realize that this proposition must sound wellnigh unintelligible to the man of today. The helpful medieval view that man is a microcosm, a reflection of the great cosmos in miniature, has long since dropped away from him, although the very existence of his world-embracing and world-conditioning psyche might have taught him better. Not only is the image of the macrocosm imprinted upon him as a psychic being, but he also creates this image for himself on an ever-widening scale. He bears this cosmic "correspondence" within him by virtue of his reflecting consciousness, on the one hand, and, on the other, thanks to the hereditary, archetypal nature of his instincts, which bind him to his environment. But his instincts not only attach him to the macrocosm; they also, in a sense, tear him apart, because his desires pull him in different directions. In this way he falls into continual conflict with himself and only very rarely succeeds in giving his life an undivided goal—for which, as a rule, he must pay very dearly by repressing other sides of his nature. One often has to ask oneself in such cases whether this kind of one-sidedness is worth forcing at all, seeing that the natural state of the human psyche consists in a certain jostling together of its components and in the contradictoriness of their behavior—that is, in a certain degree of dissociation. Buddhism calls it attachment to the "ten thousand things." Such a condition cries out for order and synthesis.

Just as the chaotic movements of the crowd,

all ending in mutual frustration, are impelled in a definite direction by a dictatorial will, so the individual in his dissociated state needs a directing and ordering principle. Ego-consciousness would like to let its own will play this role, but overlooks the existence of powerful unconscious factors which thwart its intentions. If it wants to reach the goal of synthesis, it must first get to know the nature of these factors. It must *experience* them, or else it must possess a numinous *symbol* that expresses them and conduces to synthesis. A religious symbol that comprehends and visibly represents what is seeking expression in modern man could probably do this; but our conception of the Christian symbol to date has certainly not been able to do so. On the contrary, that frightful world split runs right through the domains of the "Christian" white man, and our Christian outlook on life has proved powerless to prevent the recrudescence of an archaic social order like communism.

This is not to say that Christianity is finished. I am, on the contrary, convinced that it is not Christianity, but our conception and interpretation of it, that has become antiquated in face of the present world situation. The Christian symbol is a living thing that carries in itself the seeds of further development. It can go on developing; it depends only on us, whether we can make up our minds to meditate again, and more thoroughly, on the Christian premises. This requires a very different attitude towards the individual, towards the microcosm of the self, from the one we have had hitherto. That is why nobody knows what ways of approach are open to man, what inner experiences he can still pass through and what psychic facts underlie the religious myth. Over this hangs so universal a darkness that no one can see why he should be interested or to what end he could commit himself. Before this problem we stand helpless.

This is not surprising, since practically all the trump cards are in the hands of our opponents. They can appeal to the big battalions and their crushing power. Politics, science and technology stand ranged on their side. The imposing arguments of science represent the highest degree of intellectual certainty yet achieved by the mind of man. So at least it seems to the man of today, who has received hundred-fold enlightenment concerning the backwardness and darkness of past ages and their superstitions. That his teachers have themselves gone seriously astray by making false comparisons between incommensurable factors never enters his head. All the more so as the intellectual elite to whom he puts his questions are almost unanimously agreed that what science regards as impossible today was impossible at all other times as well. Above all, the facts of faith, which might give him the chance of an extra-mundane standpoint, are treated in the same context as the facts of science. Thus, when the individual questions the Churches and their spokesmen, to whom is entrusted the cure of souls, he is informed that membership in a creed—a decidedly worldly institution—is more or less *de rigueur* for religious belief; that the facts of faith which have become questionable for him were concrete historical events; that certain ritual actions produce miraculous effects; and that the sufferings of Christ have vicariously saved him from sin and its consequences (i.e., eternal damnation). If, with the limited means at his disposal, he begins to reflect on these things, he will have to confess that he does not understand them at all and that only two possibilities are open to him: either to believe implicitly, or to reject such statements because they are flatly incomprehensible.

Whereas the man of today can easily think

about and understand all the "truths" dished out to him by the State, his understanding of religion is made considerably more difficult owing to the lack of explanations. ("Do you understand what you are reading?" And he said, "How can I, unless some one guides me?" Acts 8:30.) If, despite this, he has still not discarded all his religious convictions, this is because the religious impulse rests on an instinctive basis and is therefore a specifically human function. You can take away a man's gods, but only to give him others in return. The leaders of the mass State cannot avoid being deified, and wherever crudities of this kind have not yet been put over by force, obsessive factors arise in their stead, charged with demonic energy— for instance, money, work, political influence, and so forth. When any natural human function gets lost, i.e., is denied conscious and intentional expression, a general disturbance results. Hence, it is quite natural that with the triumph of the Goddess of Reason a general neuroticizing of modern man should set in, a dissociation of personality analogous to the splitting of the world today by the Iron Curtain. This boundary line bristling with barbed wire runs through the psyche of modern man, no matter on which side he lives. And just as the typical neurotic is unconscious of his *shadow side,* so the normal individual, like the neurotic, sees his shadow in his neighbor or in the man beyond the great divide. It has even become a political and social duty to apostrophize the capitalism of the one and the communism of the other as the very devil, so as to fascinate the outward eye and prevent it from looking at the individual life within. But just as the neurotic, despite unconsciousness of his other side, has a dim premonition that all is not well with his psychic economy, so Western man has developed an instinctive interest in his psyche and in "psychology."

Thus it is that the doctor is summoned willynilly to appear on the world stage, and questions are addressed to him which primarily concern the most intimate and hidden life of the individual, but which in the last analysis are the direct effects of the *Zeitgeist.* Because of its personal symptomatology this material is usually considered to be "neurotic"—and rightly so, since it is made up of infantile fantasies which ill accord with the contents of an adult psyche and are therefore repressed by our moral judgment, in so far as they reach consciousness at all. Most fantasies of this kind do not, in the nature of things, come to consciousness in infantile form, and it is very improbable, to say the least of it, that they were ever conscious and were consciously repressed. Rather, they seem to have been present always, or, at any rate, to have arisen unconsciously and to have persisted in this state until the psychologist's intervention enabled them to cross the threshold of consciousness. The activation of unconscious fantasies is a process that occurs when consciousness finds itself in a critical situation. Were that not so, the fantasies would be produced normally and would then be followed by the usual neurotic disturbance. In reality, fantasies of this kind belong to the world of childhood and give rise to disturbances only when prematurely strengthened by abnormal conditions in the conscious life. This is particularly likely to happen when unfavorable influences emanate from the parents, poisoning the atmosphere and producing conflicts which upset the psychic balance of the child.

When a neurosis breaks out in an adult, the fantasy world of childhood reappears, and one is tempted to explain the onset of the neurosis causally, as due to the presence of infantile fantasies. But that does not explain why the fantasies did not develop any pathological effects during the interim period. These effects develop only when the individual comes up against a situation which he cannot overcome by conscious means. The resultant standstill in the development of personality opens a sluice for infantile fantasies, which, of course, are latent in everybody but do not display any activity so long as the conscious personality can continue on its way unimpeded. When the fantasies reach a certain level of intensity, they begin to break through into consciousness and create a conflict situation that becomes perceptible to the patient himself, splitting him into two personalities with different characters. The dissociation, however, had been prepared long before in the unconscious, when the energy flowing off from consciousness (because unused) strengthened the negative qualities of the unconscious personality, and particularly its infantile traits.

Since the normal fantasies of a child are nothing other, at bottom, than the *imagination* born of the instinctive impulses, and may thus be regarded as preliminary exercises in the use of future conscious activities, it follows that the fantasies of the neurotic, even though pathologically altered and perhaps perverted by the regression of energy, contain a core of normal instinct, the hallmark of which is adaptedness.

A neurotic illness always implies an unadapted alteration and distortion of normal dynamisms and of the "imagination" proper to them. Instincts, however, are highly conservative and of extreme antiquity as regards both their dynamism and their form. Their form, when represented to the mind, appears as an *image* which expresses the nature of the instinctive impulse visually and concretely, like a picture. If we could look into the psyche of the yucca moth,* for instance, we would find in it a pattern of ideas, of a numinous or fascinating character, which not only compel the moth to carry out its fertilizing activity on the yucca plant, but help it to "recognize" the total situation. Instinct is anything but a blind and indefinite impulse, since it proves to be attuned and adapted to a definite external situation. This latter circumstance gives it its specific and irreducible form. Just as instinct is original and hereditary, so, too, its form is age-old, that is to say, *archetypal*. It is even older and more conservative than the body's form.

These biological considerations naturally apply also to Homo sapiens, who still remains within the framework of general biology de-

* This is a classic instance of the symbiosis of insect and plant.

spite the possession of consciousness, will and reason. The fact that our conscious activity is rooted in instinct and derives from it its dynamism as well as the basic features of its ideational forms has the same significance for human psychology as for all other members of the animal kingdom. Human knowledge consists essentially in the constant adaptation of the primordial patterns of ideas that were given us a priori. These need certain modifications, because, in their original form, they are suited to an archaic mode of life but not to the demands of a specifically differentiated environment. If the flow of instinctive dynamism into our life is to be maintained, as is absolutely necessary for our existence, then it is imperative that we remold these archetypal forms into ideas which are adequate to the challenge of the present.

cannot simply be replaced by a new rational configuration, for this would be molded too much by the outer situation and not enough by man's biological needs. Moreover, not only would it build no bridge to the original man, but it would block the approach to him altogether. This is in keeping with the aims of Marxist education, which seeks, like God himself, to mold man, but in the image of the State. Today, our basic convictions have become increasingly rationalistic. Our philosophy is no longer a way of life, as it was in antiquity; it has turned into an exclusively intellectual and academic affair. Our denominational religions with their archaic rites and conceptions—justified enough in themselves—express a view of the world which caused no great difficulties in the Middle Ages but has become strange and unintelligible to the man of today. Despite this conflict with the modern scientific outlook, a deep instinct bids him hang on to ideas which, if taken literally, leave out of account all the mental developments of the last five hundred years. The obvious purpose of this is to prevent him from falling into the abyss of nihilistic despair. But even when, as rationalists, we feel impelled to criticize contemporary religion as literalistic, narrow-minded and obsolescent, we should never forget that the creeds proclaim a doctrine whose symbols, although their interpretation may be disputed, nevertheless possess a life of their own on account of their archetypal character. Consequently, intellectual understanding is by no means indispensable in all cases, but is called for only when evaluation through feeling and intuition does not suffice, that is to say, with people for whom the intellect holds the prime power of conviction.

Nothing is more characteristic and symptomatic in this respect than the gulf that has opened out between *faith* and *knowledge*. The contrast has become so enormous that one is obliged to speak of the incommensurability of these two categories and their way of looking at the world. And yet they are concerned with the same empirical world in which we live, for even theology tells us that faith is supported by facts that became historically perceptible in this known world of ours, namely, that Christ was born as a real human being, worked many miracles and suffered his fate, died under Pontius Pilate and rose up in the flesh after his death. Theology rejects any tendency to take the statements of its earliest records as written myths and, accordingly, to understand them symbolically. Indeed, it is the theologians themselves who have recently made the attempt—no doubt as a concession to "knowledge"—to "demythologize" the object of their faith while drawing the line quite arbitrarily at the crucial points. But to the critical intellect it is only too obvious that myth is an integral component of all religions and therefore cannot be excluded from the assertions of faith without injuring them.

The rupture between faith and knowledge is a symptom of the *split consciousness* which is so characteristic of the mental disorder of our day. It is as if two different persons were making statements about the same thing, each from his own point of view, or as if one person in two different frames of mind were sketching a picture of his experience. If for "person" we substitute "modern society," it is evident that the latter is suffering from a mental dissociation, i.e., a neurotic disturbance. In view of this, it does not help matters at all if one party pulls obstinately to the right and the other to the left. This is what happens in every neurotic psyche, to its own deep distress, and it is just this distress that brings the patient to the doctor.

As I stated above in all brevity—while not

neglecting to mention certain practical details whose omission might have perplexed the reader—the doctor has to establish a relationship with *both* halves of his patient's personality, because only from them both, and not merely from one half with the suppression of the other, can he put together a whole and complete man. The latter alternative is what the patient has been doing all along, for the modern *Weltanschauung* gives him no other guidance. His individual situation is the same in principle as the collective situation. He is a social microcosm, reflecting on the smallest scale the quantities of society at large, or, conversely, as the smallest social unit, cumulatively producing the collective dissociation. The latter possibility is the more likely one, as the only direct and concrete carrier of life is the individual personality, while society and the State are conventional ideas and can claim reality only in so far as they are represented by a certain number of individuals.

Far too little attention has been paid to the fact that our age, for all its irreligiousness, is hereditarily burdened with the specific achievement of the Christian epoch: *the supremacy of the word,* of the Logos, which stands for the central figure of our Christian faith. The word has literally become our god and so it has remained, even if we know of Christianity only from hearsay. Words like "society" and "State" are so concretized that they are almost personified. In the opinion of the man in the street, the "State," far more than any king in history, is the inexhaustible giver of all good; the "State" is invoked, made responsible, grumbled at, and so on and so forth. Society is elevated to the rank of a supreme ethical principle; indeed, it is credited with positively creative capacities.

No one seems to notice that the veneration of the word, which was necessary for a certain phase of historical development, has a perilous shadow side. That is to say, the moment the word, as a result of centuries of education, attains universal validity, it severs its original link with the divine person. There is then a personified Church, a personified State; belief in the word becomes credulity, and the word itself an infernal slogan capable of any deception. With credulity come propaganda and advertising to dupe the citizen with political jobbery and compromises, and the lie reaches proportions never known before in the history of the world.

Thus, the word, originally announcing the

unity of all men and their union in the figure of the one great Man, has in our day become the source of suspicion and distrust of all against all. Credulity is one of our worst enemies, but that is the makeshift the neurotic always resorts to in order to quell the doubter in his own breast or conjure him out of existence. People think you have only to "tell" a person that he "ought" to do something in order to put him on the right track. But whether he can or will do it is another matter. The psychologist has come to see that nothing is achieved by telling, persuading, admonishing, giving good advice. He must also get acquainted with the details and have an authentic knowledge of the psychic inventory of his patient. He has therefore to relate to the individuality of the sufferer and feel his way into all the nooks and crannies of his mind, to a degree that far exceeds the capacity of a teacher or even of a *directeur de conscience*. His scientific objectivity, which excludes nothing, enables him to see his patient not only as a human being but also as a subhuman who is bound to his body, like an animal. The development of science has directed his interest beyond the range of the conscious personality to the world of unconscious instinct dominated by sexuality and the power drive (or self-assertion) corresponding to the twin moral concepts of Saint Augustine: *concupiscentia* and *superbia*. The clash between these two fundamental instincts (preservation of the species and self-preservation) is the source of numerous conflicts. They are, therefore, the chief object of moral judgment, whose purpose it is to prevent these instinctual collisions as far as possible.

As I explained above, instinct has two main aspects: on the one hand, that of dynamism, drive or drift, and on the other, specific meaning and intention. It is highly probable that all man's psychic functions have an instinctual foundation, as is obviously the case with animals. It is easy to see that in animals instinct functions as the *spiritus rector* of all their behavior. This observation lacks certainty only where the learning capacity begins to develop, for instance in the higher apes and in man. In the animals, as a result of their learning capacity, instinct undergoes numerous modifications and differentiations; in civilized man the instincts are so split up that only a few of the basic ones can be recognized with any certainty in their original form. The most important are the two fundamental instincts and their derivatives, and these have been the exclusive concern of medical psychology so far. Investigators found, however, that in following up the ramifications of the instincts they hit upon configurations which could not with certainty be ascribed to either group. To take but one example: the discoverer of the power instinct was in some doubt as to whether an apparently indubitable expression of the sexual instinct might not be better explained as a "power arrangement," and Freud himself felt obliged to acknowledge the existence of "ego instincts" in addition to the overriding sex instinct—a clear concession to the Adlerian standpoint. In view of this uncertainty, it is hardly surprising that in most cases neurotic symptoms can be explained, almost without contradiction, in terms of either theory. This perplexity does not mean that one or the other standpoint, or both of them, is erroneous. Rather, they are both *relatively* valid and, unlike certain one-sided and dogmatic preferences, allow the existence and competition of other instincts. Although, as I have said, the question of human instinct is a far from simple matter, we shall probably not be wrong in assuming that the learning capacity, a quality almost exclusive to man, is based on the instinct for imitation found in animals. It is in

the nature of this instinct to disturb other
instinctive activities and eventually to modify
them, as can be observed, for instance, in the
songs of birds, when they adopt other melo-
dies.

Nothing estranges man more from the
ground plan of his instincts than his learning
capacity, which turns out to be a genuine drive
towards progressive transformations of human
modes of behavior. It, more than anything else,
is responsible for the altered conditions of our
existence and the need for new adaptations
which civilization brings. It is also the source
of numerous psychic disturbances and difficulties occasioned by man's progressive alienation
from his instinctual foundation, i.e., by his
*uprootedness* and identification with his conscious knowledge of himself, by his concern
with consciousness at the expense of the unconscious. The result is that modern man can
know himself only in so far as he can become
conscious of himself—a capacity largely dependent on environmental conditions, the
drive for knowledge and control of which ne-
cessitated or suggested certain modifications of
his original instinctive tendencies. His consciousness therefore orients itself chiefly by
observing and investigating the world around

him, and it is to its peculiarities that he must adapt his psychic and technical resources. This task is so exacting, and its fulfillment so advantageous, that he forgets himself in the process, losing sight of his instinctual nature and putting his own conception of himself in place of his real being. In this way he slips imperceptibly into a purely conceptual world where the products of his conscious activity progressively replace reality.

Separation from his instinctual nature inevitably plunges civilized man into the conflict between conscious and unconscious, spirit and nature, knowledge and faith, a split that becomes pathological the moment his consciousness is no longer able to neglect or suppress his instinctual side. The accumulation of individuals who have got into this critical state starts off a mass movement purporting to be the champion of the suppressed. In accordance with the prevailing tendency of consciousness to seek the source of all ills in the outside world, the cry goes up for political and social changes which, it is supposed, would automatically solve the much deeper problem of split personality. Hence it is that whenever this demand is fulfilled, political and social conditions arise which bring the same ills back again in altered form. What then happens is a simple reversal: the underside comes to the top and the shadow takes the place of the light, and since the former is always anarchic and turbulent, the freedom of the "liberated" underdog must suffer Draconian curtailment. All this is unavoidable, because the root of the evil is untouched and merely the counterposition has come to light.

The Communist revolution has debased man far lower than democratic collective psychology has done, because it robs him of his freedom not only in the social but in the moral and spiritual sense. Aside from the political difficulties, the West has suffered a great psychological disadvantage that made itself unpleasantly felt even in the days of German Nazism: the existence of a dictator allows us to point the finger away from ourselves and at the shadow. He is clearly on the other side of the political frontier, while we are on the side of good and enjoy the possession of the right ideal. Did not a well-known statesman recently confess that he had "no imagination in evil"? In the name of the multitude he was here giving expression to the fact that Western man is in danger of losing his shadow altogether, of identifying himself with his fictive personality and of identifying the world with the abstract picture painted by scientific rationalism. His spiritual and moral opponent, who is just as real as he, no longer dwells in his own breast but beyond the geographical line of division, which no longer represents an outward political barrier but splits off the conscious from the unconscious man more and more menacingly. Thinking and feeling lose their inner polarity, and where religious orientation has grown ineffective, not even a god is at hand to check the sovereign sway of unleashed psychic functions.

Our rational philosophy does not bother itself with whether the other person in us, pejoratively described as the "shadow," is in sympathy with our conscious plans and intentions. Evidently it does not know that we carry in ourselves a real shadow whose existence is grounded in our instinctual nature. The dynamism and imagery of the instincts together form an a priori which no man can overlook without the gravest risk to himself. Violation or neglect of instinct has painful consequences of a physiological and psychological nature for whose removal medical help, above all, is required.

For more than fifty years we have known,

or could have known, that there is an unconscious as a counterbalance to consciousness. Medical psychology has furnished all the necessary empirical and experimental proofs of this. There is an unconscious psychic reality which demonstrably influences consciousness and its contents. All this is known, but no practical conclusions have been drawn from it. We still go on thinking and acting as before, as if we were *simplex* and not *duplex*. Accordingly, we imagine ourselves to be innocuous, reasonable and humane. We do not think of distrusting our motives or of asking ourselves how the inner man feels about the things we do in the outside world. But actually it is frivolous, superficial and unreasonable of us, as well as psychically unhygienic, to overlook the reaction and standpoint of the unconscious. One can regard one's stomach or heart as unimportant and worthy of contempt, but that does not prevent overeating or overexertion from having consequences that affect the whole man. Yet we think that psychic mistakes and their consequences can be got rid of with mere words, for "psychic" means less than air to most people. All the same, nobody can deny that without the psyche there would be no world at all, and still less, a human world.

Virtually everything depends on the human soul and its functions. It should be worthy of all the attention we can give it, especially today, when everyone admits that the weal or woe of the future will be decided neither by the attacks of wild animals nor by natural catastrophes nor by the danger of world-wide epidemics but simply and solely by the psychic changes in man. It needs only an almost imperceptible disturbance of equilibrium in a few of our rulers' heads to plunge the world into blood, fire and radioactivity. The technical means necessary for this are present on both sides. And certain conscious deliberations, uncontrolled by any inner opponent, can be indulged in all too easily, as we have seen already from the example of one "Leader." The consciousness of modern man still clings so much to outward objects that he makes them exclusively responsible, as if it were on them that the decision depended. That the psychic state of certain individuals could emancipate itself for once from the behavior of objects is something that is considered far too little, although irrationalities of this sort are observed every day and can happen to everyone.

The forlornness of consciousness in our world is due primarily to the loss of instinct, and the reason for this lies in the development of the human mind over the past aeon. The more power man had over nature, the more his knowledge and skill went to his head, and the deeper became his contempt for the merely natural and accidental, for that which is irrationally given—including the objective psyche, which is all that consciousness is not. In contrast to the subjectivism of the conscious mind the unconscious is objective, manifesting itself mainly in the form of contrary feelings, fantasies, emotions, impulses and dreams, none of which one makes oneself but which come upon one objectively. Even today psychology is still, for the most part, the science of conscious contents, measured as far as possible by collective standards. The individual psyche has become a mere accident, a "random" phenomenon, while the unconscious, which can manifest itself only in the real, "irrationally given" human being, has been ignored altogether. This was not the result of carelessness or of lack of knowledge, but of downright resistance to the mere possibility of there being a second psychic authority besides the ego. It seems a positive menace to the ego that its monarchy can be doubted. The religious person, on the other hand, is accustomed to the thought of not being sole master in his own house. He believes that God, and not he himself, decides in the end. But how many of us would dare to let the will of God decide, and which of us would not feel embarrassed if he had to say how far the decision came from God himself?

The religious person, so far as one can judge, stands directly under the influence of the reaction from the unconscious. As a rule, he calls this the operation of *conscience*. But since the same psychic background produces reactions other than moral ones, the believer is measuring his conscience by the traditional ethical standard and thus by a collective value, in which endeavor he is assiduously supported by his Church. So long as the individual can hold fast to his traditional beliefs, and the circumstances of his time do not demand stronger emphasis on individual autonomy, he can rest content with the situation. But the situation is radically altered when the worldly-minded man who is oriented to external factors and has lost his religious beliefs appears en masse, as is the case today. The believer is then forced onto the defensive and must catechize himself on the foundation of his beliefs. He is no longer sustained by the tremendous suggestive power of the *consensus omnium*,

and is keenly aware of the weakening of the
Church and the precariousness of its dogmatic
assumptions. To counter this, the Church rec-
ommends more faith, as if this gift of grace depended on man's good will and pleasure. The
seat of faith, however, is not consciousness but
spontaneous religious experience, which brings
the individual's faith into immediate relation
with God.

Here we must ask: Have I any religious experience and immediate relation to God, and
hence that certainty which will keep me, as an
individual, from dissolving in the crowd?

# VI

## SELF-KNOWLEDGE

To THIS QUESTION THERE IS A POSITIVE AN-
swer only when the individual is willing to
fulfill the demands of rigorous self-examina-
tion and self-knowledge. If he follows through
his intention, he will not only discover some
important truths about himself, but will also
have gained a psychological advantage: he will
have succeeded in deeming himself worthy of
serious attention and sympathetic interest. He
will have set his hand, as it were, to a declara-
tion of his own human dignity and taken the
first step towards the foundations of his consciousness—that is, towards the unconscious,
the only accessible source of religious experience. This is certainly not to say that what we
call the unconscious is identical with God or is

set up in his place. It is the medium from which the religious experience seems to flow. As to what the further cause of such an experience may be, the answer to this lies beyond the range of human knowledge. Knowledge of God is a transcendental problem.

The religious person enjoys a great advantage when it comes to answering the crucial question that hangs over our time like a threat: he has a clear idea of the way his subjective existence is grounded in his relation to "God." I put the word "God" in quotes in order to indicate that we are dealing with an anthropomorphic idea whose dynamism and symbolism are filtered through the medium of the unconscious psyche. Anyone who wants to can at least draw near to the source of such experiences, no matter whether he believes in God or not. Without this approach it is only in rare cases that we witness those miraculous conversions of which Paul's Damascus experience is the prototype. That religious experiences exist no longer needs proof. But it will always remain doubtful whether what metaphysics and theology call God and the gods is the real ground of these experiences. The question is idle, actually, and answers itself by reason of the subjectively overwhelming numinosity of the experience. Anyone who has had it is *seized* by it and therefore not in a position to indulge in fruitless metaphysical or epistemological speculations. Absolute certainty brings its own evidence and has no need of anthropomorphic proofs.

In view of the general ignorance of and bias against psychology it must be accounted a misfortune that the one experience which makes sense of individual existence should seem to have its origin in a medium that is certain to catch everybody's prejudices. Once more the doubt is heard: "What good can come out of Nazareth?" The unconscious, if not regarded outright as a sort of refuse bin underneath the conscious mind, is at any rate supposed to be of "merely animal nature." In reality, however, and by definition it is of uncertain extent and constitution, so that overvaluation or undervaluation of it is groundless and can be dismissed as mere prejudice. At all events, such judgments sound very queer in the mouths of Christians, whose Lord was himself born on the straw of a stable, among the domestic animals. It would have been more to the taste of the multitude if he had got himself born in a temple. In the same way, the worldly-minded mass man looks for the numinous experience in the mass meeting, which provides an infinitely more imposing background than the individual soul. Even Church Christians share this pernicious delusion.

Psychology's insistence on the importance of unconscious processes for religious experience is extremely unpopular, no less with the political Right than with the Left. For the former the deciding factor is the historical revelation that came to man from outside; to the latter this is sheer nonsense, and man has no religious function at all, except belief in the party doctrine, when suddenly the most intense faith is called for. On top of this, the various creeds assert quite different things, and each of them claims to possess the absolute truth. Yet today we live in a unitary world where distances are reckoned by hours and no longer by weeks and months. Exotic races have ceased to be peepshows in ethnological museums. They have become our neighbors, and what was yesterday the prerogative of the ethnologist is today a political, social and psychological problem. Already the ideological spheres begin to touch, to interpenetrate, and the time may not be so far off when the question of mutual understanding in this field will become acute. To make oneself understood is certainly impossible without far-reaching comprehension of the other's standpoint. The insight needed for this will have repercussions on both sides. History will undoubtedly pass over those who feel it is their vocation to resist this inevitable development, however desirable and psychologically necessary it may be to cling to what is essential and good in our own tradition. Despite all the differences, the unity of mankind will assert itself irresistibly. On this card Marxist doctrine has staked its life, while the West hopes to get by with technology and economic aid. Communism has not overlooked the enormous importance of the ideological element and the universality of basic principles. The nations of the Far East share our ideological weakness and are just as vulnerable as we are.

The underestimation of the psychological factor is likely to take a bitter revenge. It is therefore high time we caught up with ourselves in this matter. For the present this must remain a pious wish, because self-knowledge, as well as being highly unpopular, seems to be an unpleasantly idealistic goal, reeks of morality, and is preoccupied with the psychological shadow, which is normally denied whenever possible or at least not spoken of. The task that faces our age is indeed almost insuperably difficult. It makes the highest demands on our responsibility if we are not to be guilty of another *trahison des clercs*. It addresses itself to those guiding and influential personalities who have the necessary intelligence to understand the situation our world is in. One might expect them to consult their consciences. But since it is a matter not only of intellectual understanding but of moral conclusions, there is unfortunately no cause for optimism. Nature, as we know, is not so lavish with her boons that she joins to a high intelligence the gifts of the heart also. As a rule, where one is present the other is lacking, and where one capacity is present in perfection it is generally at the cost of all the others. The discrepancy between intellect and feeling, which get in each other's way at the best of times, is a particularly painful chapter in the history of the human psyche.

There is no sense in formulating the task that our age has forced upon us as a moral demand. We can, at best, merely make the psychological world situation so clear that it can be seen even by the myopic, and give utterance to words and ideas which even the hard of hearing can hear. We may hope for men of understanding and men of good will, and must therefore not grow weary of reiterating those thoughts and insights which are needed. Finally, even the truth can spread and not only the popular lie.

With these words I should like to draw the reader's attention to the main difficulty he has to face. The horror which the dictator States have of late brought upon mankind is nothing less than the culmination of all those atrocities of which our ancestors made themselves guilty in the not so distant past. Quite apart from the barbarities and blood baths perpetrated by the Christian nations among themselves throughout European history, the European has also to answer for all the crimes he has committed against the dark-skinned peoples during the process of colonization. In this respect the white man carries a very heavy burden indeed. It shows us a picture of the common human shadow that could hardly be painted in blacker colors. The evil that comes to light in man and that undoubtedly dwells within him is of gigantic proportions, so that for the Church to talk of original sin and to trace it back to Adam's relatively innocent slip-up with Eve is almost a euphemism. The case is far graver and is grossly underestimated.

Since it is universally believed that man *is*

merely what his consciousness knows of itself, he regards himself as harmless and so adds stupidity to iniquity. He does not deny that terrible things have happened and still go on happening, but it is always "the others" who do them. And when such deeds belong to the recent or remote past, they quickly and conveniently sink into the sea of forgetfulness, and that state of chronic woolly-mindedness returns which we describe as "normality." In shocking contrast to this is the fact that nothing has finally disappeared and nothing has been made good. The evil, the guilt, the profound unease of conscience, the obscure misgiving are there before our eyes, if only we would see. Man has done these things; I am a man, who has his share of human nature; therefore I am guilty with the rest and bear unaltered and indelibly within me the capacity and the inclination to do them again at any time. Even if, juristically speaking, we were not accessories to the crime, we are always, thanks to our human nature, potential criminals. In reality we merely lacked a suitable opportunity to be drawn into the infernal melee. None of us stands outside humanity's black collective shadow. Whether the crime lies many generations back or happens today, it remains the symptom of a disposition that is always and everywhere present—and one would therefore do well to possess some "imagination in evil," for only the fool can permanently neglect the conditions of his own nature. In fact, this negligence is the best means of making him an instrument of evil. Harmlessness and naiveté are as little helpful as it would be for a cholera patient and those in his vicinity to remain unconscious of the contagiousness of the disease. On the contrary, they lead to projection of the unrecognized evil into the "other." This strengthens the opponent's position in the most effective way, because the projection carries the *fear* which we involuntarily and secretly feel for our own evil over to the other side and considerably increases the formidableness of his threat. What is even worse, our lack of insight deprives us of the *capacity to deal with evil*. Here, of course, we come up against one of the main prejudices of the Christian tradition, and one that is a great stumbling block to our policies. We should, so we are told, eschew evil and, if possible, neither touch nor mention it. For evil is also the thing of ill omen, that which is tabooed and feared. This attitude towards evil, and the apparent circumventing of it, flatter the primitive tendency in us to shut our eyes to evil and drive it over some frontier or other, like the Old Testament scapegoat, which was supposed to carry the evil into the wilderness.

But if one can no longer avoid the realization that evil, without man's ever having chosen it, is lodged in human nature itself, then it bestrides the psychological stage as the equal and opposite partner of good. This realization leads straight to a psychological dualism, already unconsciously prefigured in the political world schism and in the even more unconscious dissociation in modern man himself. The dualism does not come from this realization; rather, we are in a split condition to begin with. It would be an insufferable thought that we had to take personal responsibility for so much guiltiness. We therefore prefer to localize the evil with individual criminals or groups of criminals, while washing our hands in innocence and ignoring the general proclivity to evil. This sanctimoniousness cannot be kept up, in the long run, because the evil, as experience shows, lies in man— unless, in accordance with the Christian view, one is willing to postulate a metaphysical principle of evil. The great advantage of this view is that it exonerates man's conscience of too heavy a responsibility and fobs it off on the devil, in correct psychological appreciation of the fact that man is much more the victim of his psychic constitution than its inventor. Considering that the evil of our day puts everything that has ever agonized mankind in the deepest shade, one must ask oneself how it is that, for all our progress in the administration of justice, in medicine and in technology, for all our concern for life and health, monstrous engines of destruction have been invented which could easily exterminate the human race.

No one will maintain that the atomic physicists are a pack of criminals because it is to their efforts that we owe that peculiar flower of human ingenuity, the hydrogen bomb. The vast amount of intellectual work that went into the development of nuclear physics was put forth by men who devoted themselves to their task with the greatest exertions and self-sacrifice and whose moral achievement could just as easily have earned them the merit of inventing something useful and beneficial to humanity. But even though the first step along the road to a momentous invention may be the outcome of a conscious decision, here, as everywhere, the spontaneous idea—the hunch or intuition—plays an important part. In other words, the unconscious collaborates too and often makes decisive contributions. So it is not the conscious effort alone that is responsible for the result; somewhere or other the unconscious, with its barely discernible goals and intentions, has its finger in the pie. If it puts a weapon in your hand, it is aiming at some kind of violence. Knowledge of the truth is the foremost goal of science, and if in pursuit of the longing for light we stumble upon an immense danger, then one has the impression more of fatality than of premeditation. It is not that present-day man is capable of greater evil than the man of antiquity or the primitive. He merely has incomparably more effective means with which to realize his proclivity to evil. As his consciousness has broadened and differentiated, so his moral nature has lagged behind. That is the great problem before us today. *Reason alone does not suffice.*

In theory, it lies within the power of reason to desist from experiments of such hellish scope as nuclear fission if only because of their dangerousness. But fear of the evil which one does not see in one's own bosom but always in somebody else's checks reason every time, although one knows that the use of this weapon means the certain end of our present human world. The fear of universal destruction may spare us the worst, yet the possibility of it will nevertheless hang over us like a dark cloud so long as no bridge is found across the world-wide psychic and political split—a bridge as certain as the existence of the hydrogen bomb. If a world-wide consciousness could arise that all division and all antagonism are due to the splitting of opposites in the psyche, then one would really know where to attack. But if even the smallest and most personal stirrings of the individual soul—so insignificant in themselves —remain as unconscious and unrecognized as they have hitherto, they will go on accumulating and produce mass groupings and mass movements which cannot be subjected to reasonable control or manipulated to a good end. All direct efforts to do so are no more than shadow boxing, the most infatuated by illusion being the gladiators themselves.

The deciding factor lies with the individual man, who knows no answer to his dualism. This abyss has suddenly yawned open before him with the latest events in world history, after mankind had lived for many centuries in the comfortable belief that a unitary God had created man in his own image, as a little unity. Even today people are largely unconscious of the fact that every individual is a cell in the structure of various international organisms and is therefore causally implicated in their conflicts. The individual man knows that as an individual being he is more or less meaningless and feels himself the victim of uncontrollable forces, but, on the other hand, he harbors within himself a dangerous shadow and opponent who is involved as an invisible helper in the dark machinations of the political monster. It is in the nature of political bodies always to see the evil in the opposite group, just as the individual has an ineradicable tendency to get rid of everything he does not know and does not want to know about himself by foisting it off on somebody else.

Nothing has a more divisive and alienating effect upon society than this moral complacency and lack of responsibility, and nothing promotes understanding and *rapprochement* more than the mutual withdrawal of projections. This necessary corrective requires self-criticism, for one cannot just tell the other person to withdraw them. He does not recognize them for what they are, any more than one does oneself. We can recognize our prejudices and illusions only when, from a broader psychological knowledge of ourselves and others, we are prepared to doubt the absolute rightness of our assumptions and compare them carefully and conscientiously with the objective facts. Funnily enough, "self-criticism" is an idea much in vogue in Marxist countries, but there it is subordinated to ideological considerations and must serve the State, and not truth and justice in men's dealings with one another. The mass State has no intention of promoting mutual understanding and the relationship of man to man; it strives, rather, for atomization, for the psychic isolation of the individual. The more unrelated individuals are, the more consolidated the State becomes, and vice versa.

There can be no doubt that in the democracies too the distance between man and man is much greater than is conducive to public welfare or beneficial to our psychic needs. True, all sorts of attempts are being made to level out glaring social contrasts by appealing to people's idealism, enthusiasm and ethical conscience; but, characteristically, one forgets to apply the necessary self-criticism, to answer the question: *Who* is making the idealistic demand? Is it, perchance, someone who jumps over his own shadow in order to hurl himself avidly on an idealistic program that promises him a welcome alibi? How much respectability and apparent morality is there, cloaking with deceptive colors a very different inner world of darkness? One would first like to be assured that the man who talks of ideals is himself ideal, so that his words and deeds *are* more than they *seem*. To be ideal is impossible, and remains therefore an unfulfilled postulate. Since we usually have keen noses in this respect, most of the idealisms that are preached and paraded before us sound rather hollow and become acceptable only when their opposite is openly admitted to. Without this counterweight the ideal goes beyond our human capacity, becomes incredible because of its humorlessness and degenerates into bluff, albeit a well-meant one. Bluff is an illegitimate way of overpowering and suppressing people and leads to no good.

Recognition of the shadow, on the other hand, leads to the modesty we need in order to acknowledge imperfection. And it is just this conscious recognition and consideration that are needed wherever a human relationship is to be established. A human relationship is not based on differentiation and perfection, for these only emphasize the differences or call forth the exact opposite; it is based, rather, on imperfection, on what is weak, helpless and in need of support—the very ground and motive of dependence. The perfect has no need of the other, but weakness has, for it seeks support and does not confront its partner with anything that might force him into an inferior position and even humiliate him. This humiliation may happen only too easily where idealism plays too prominent a role.

Reflections of this kind should not be taken as superfluous sentimentalities. The question of human relationship and of the inner cohesion of our society is an urgent one in view of the atomization of the pent-up mass man, whose personal relationships are undermined by general mistrust. Wherever justice is uncertain and police spying and terror are at work, human beings fall into isolation, which, of course, is the aim and purpose of the dictator State, since it is based on the greatest possible accumulation of depotentiated social units. To counter this danger, the free society needs a bond of an affective nature, a principle of a kind like *caritas,* the Christian love of your neighbor. But it is just this love for one's fellow man that suffers most of all from the lack of understanding wrought by projection. It would therefore be very much in the interest of the free society to give some thought to the question of human relationship from the psychological point of view, for in this resides its real cohesion and consequently its strength. Where love stops, power begins, and violence, and terror.

These reflections are not intended as an appeal to idealism, but only to heighten the consciousness of the psychological situation. I do not know which is weaker: idealism or the insight of the public. I only know that it needs time to bring about psychic changes that have any prospect of enduring. Insight that dawns slowly seems to me to have more lasting effects than a fitful idealism, which is unlikely to hold out for long.

# VII

## THE MEANING OF SELF-KNOWLEDGE

WHAT OUR AGE THINKS OF AS THE "SHADOW" and inferior part of the psyche contains more than something merely negative. The very fact that through self-knowledge, i.e., by exploring our own souls, we come upon the instincts and their world of imagery should throw some light on the powers slumbering in the psyche, of which we are seldom aware so long as all goes well. They are potentialities of the greatest dynamism, and it depends entirely on the preparedness and attitude of the conscious mind whether the irruption of these forces and the images and ideas associated with them will tend towards construction or catastrophe. The psychologist seems to be the only person who knows from experience how precarious the psychic preparedness of modern man is, for he is the only one who sees himself compelled to seek out in man's nature those helpful forces and ideas which over and over have enabled the individual to find the right way through darkness and danger. For this exacting work the psychologist requires all his patience; he may not rely on any traditional "ought's" and "must's," leaving the other person to make all the effort and contenting himself with the easy role of adviser and admonisher. Everyone knows the futility of preaching about things that are desirable, yet the general helplessness in this situation is so great, and the need so dire, that one prefers to repeat the old mistake instead of racking one's brains over a subjective problem. Besides, it is always a question of treating one single individual only and not ten thousand, where the trouble one takes would ostensibly have more impressive results, though one knows well enough that nothing has happened at all unless the individual changes.

The effect on *all* individuals, which one would like to see realized, may not set in for hundreds of years, for the spiritual transformation of mankind follows the slow tread of the centuries and cannot be hurried or held up by any rational process of reflection, let alone brought to fruition in one generation. What does lie within our reach, however, is the change in individuals who have, or create, an opportunity to influence others of like mind in their circle of acquaintance. I do not mean by persuading or preaching—I am thinking, rather, of the well-known fact that anyone who has insight into his own action, and has thus found access to the unconscious, involuntarily exercises an influence on his environment. The deepening and broadening of his consciousness produce the kind of effect which the primitives call "mana." It is an unintentional influence on the unconscious of others, a sort of unconscious prestige, and its effect lasts only so long as it is not disturbed by conscious intention.

Nor does the striving for self-knowledge altogether shun the prospect of social amelioration, since there exists a factor which, though completely disregarded, meets our expectations halfway. This is the unconscious *Zeitgeist*. It compensates the attitude of the conscious mind and anticipates changes to come. An excellent example of this is modern art: though seeming to deal with aesthetic problems, it is really performing a work of psychological education on the public by breaking down and destroying their previous aesthetic views of what is beautiful in form and meaningful in content. The pleasingness of the artistic product is replaced by chill abstractions of the most subjective nature which brusquely slam the door on the naive and romantic delight in the senses and their obligatory love for the object. This tells us, in plain and universal language, that the prophetic spirit of art has turned away from the old object relationship and towards the—for the time being—dark chaos of subjectivisms. Certainly art, so far as we can judge of it, has not yet discovered in this darkness what it is that holds all men together and could give expression to their psychic wholeness. Since reflection seems to be needed for this purpose, it may be that such discoveries are reserved for other fields of endeavor.

Great art till now has always derived its fruitfulness from the myth, from the unconscious process of symbolization which continues through the ages and which, as the primordial manifestation of the human spirit, will continue to be the root of all creation in the future. The development of modern art with its seemingly nihilistic trend towards disintegration must be understood as the symptom and symbol of a mood of world destruction and world renewal that has set its mark on our age. This mood makes itself felt everywhere, politically, socially and philosophically. We are living in what the Greeks called the Καιρός—the right time—for a "metamorphosis of the gods," i.e., of the fundamental principles and symbols. This peculiarity of our time, which is certainly not of our conscious choosing, is the expression of the unconscious man within us who is changing. Coming generations will have to take account of this momentous transformation if humanity is not to destroy itself through the might of its own technology and science.

As at the beginning of the Christian Era, so again today we are faced with the problem of the moral backwardness which has failed to keep pace with our scientific, technical and social developments. So much is at stake and so much depends on the psychological constitution of modern man. Is he capable of resisting the temptation to use his power for the purpose of staging a world conflagration? Is he conscious of the path he is treading, and what the conclusions are that must be drawn from the present world situation and his own psychic situation? Does he know that he is on the point of losing the life-preserving myth of the inner man which Christianity has treasured up for him? Does he realize what lies in store should this catastrophe ever befall him? Is he even capable at all of realizing that this would be a catastrophe? And finally, does the individual know that *he* is the makeweight that tips the scales?

Happiness and contentment, equability of soul and meaningfulness of life—these can be experienced only by the individual and not by a State, which, on the one hand, is nothing but a convention of independent individuals and, on the other, continually threatens to paralyze and suppress the individual. The psychiatrist is one of those who know most about the conditions of the soul's welfare, upon which so infinitely much depends in the social sum. The social and political circumstances of the time are certainly of considerable significance, but their importance for the weal or woe of the individual has been boundlessly overestimated in so far as they are taken for the sole deciding factors. In this respect all our social goals commit the error of overlooking the psychology of the person for whom they are intended and—very often—of promoting only his illusions.

I hope, therefore, that a psychiatrist, who in the course of a long life has devoted himself to the causes and consequences of psychic disorders, may be permitted to express his opinion, in all the modesty enjoined upon him as an individual, about the questions raised by the world situation today. I am neither spurred on by excessive optimism nor in love with high ideals, but am merely concerned with the fate of the individual human being—that infinitesimal unit on whom a world depends, and in whom, if we read the meaning of the Christian message aright, even God seeks his goal.

## Other MENTOR Books of Special Interest

☐ **THE INDIVIDUAL AND THE CROWD: A STUDY OF IDEN-TITY IN AMERICA by Hendrik M. Ruitenbeek.** A distinguished sociologist and psychoanalyst surveys the areas in which Americans have failed to relate to their environment, and the consequences of this identity crisis.
(#MQ849—95¢)

☐ **THE BOOK OF THE IT by Georg Groddeck.** An early classic of psychoanalysis by a friend and contemporary of Freud. With an Introduction by Ashley Montagu.
(#MT352—75¢)

☐ **MALE AND FEMALE by Margaret Mead.** Explores the sexual patterns of modern men and women and discusses childhood, love and marriage in the South Seas and America.
(#MT555—75¢)

☐ **GROWING UP IN NEW GUINEA by Margaret Mead.** This study of primitive childhood throws light on problems of life today.
(#MP368—60¢)

☐ **SEX AND TEMPERAMENT IN THREE PRIMITIVE SO-CIETIES by Margaret Mead.** An investigation of the question of which personality differences between men and women are linked to their sex.
(#MP370—60¢)

☐ **HUMAN TYPES by Raymond Firth.** An introduction to social anthropology, analyzing types of mankind and his societies—their origins, differences and similarities.
(#MT590—75¢)

☐ **MAN MAKES HIMSELF by V. Gordon Childe.** Man's social and technical evolution through 350,000 years of progress.
(#MT834—75¢)